Allen Ziegler
Apt 325
1900 Trolley Rd
York, PA 17408

IMAGES
of America

OIL BOOM ARCHITECTURE
TITUSVILLE, PITHOLE, AND PETROLEUM CENTER

TITUSVILLE, NOS. 102–108 NORTH FRANKLIN STREET, STAGE ONE. A three-story frame hotel building on this site in 1864 was renamed the Mansion House in 1868. This buff brick building by architect Charles W. Terry replaced it in 1897. The massive walls and heavy bands of ornamental tile give it a Romanesque look, but the use of classical details probably qualifies it as Queen Anne. Renamed the Colonel Drake Hotel in 1946, it continued for another 50 years, until the building was demolished in 1998. (Drake Well Museum.)

On the cover: **NO. 610 NORTH PERRY STREET, TITUSVILLE.** This detailed Italianate house was built in 1873 for John Eaton, an oil producer and dealer in oil well supplies. The woodwork of the window frames and cornice was painted in contrasting colors to emphasize its variety. (Drake Well Museum.)

IMAGES
of America

OIL BOOM
ARCHITECTURE

TITUSVILLE, PITHOLE, AND
PETROLEUM CENTER

William B. Moore and Joshua F. Sherretts

ARCADIA
PUBLISHING

Published by Arcadia Publishing
Charleston, South Carolina

Library of Congress Catalog Card Number: 2007941110

For all general information contact Arcadia Publishing at:
Telephone 843-853-2070
Fax 843-853-0044
E-mail sales@arcadiapublishing.com
For customer service and orders:
Toll-Free 1-888-313-2665

Visit us on the Internet at www.arcadiapublishing.com

*To Francis J. and M. J. Moore, Bill Moore's parents, who celebrated their
anniversaries in the 1960s with lunch at the Colonel Drake Hotel
and a drive around town to look at houses, which introduced him to
Titusville architecture, and Alice E. Morrison, without whose interest in
oil region history and patient research into its details,
this book would not have been possible.*

CONTENTS

ACKNOWLEDGMENTS

As publication projects go, this has not been a large one, but many people have made it possible. At the top of the list is Drake Well Museum, Titusville, which allowed us to make use of many photographs from its collection of historic images. Barbara T. Zolli, director, and Susan J. Beates, curator, were gracious, patient, and helpful, even in the middle of Drake Well's third reaccreditation and preparations for a major remodeling. All uncredited images are from William B. Moore's personal collection.

Of critical importance in the Drake Well collection was the work of two people. The first was John A. Mather (1829–1915), who traveled throughout the Oil Creek valley with his camera and cumbersome equipment, documenting all of the early oil towns. Miraculously, almost 3,400 of his glass plate negatives survived and are in the collection of the Drake Well Museum. The second was Elizabeth E. (Fletcher) Hequembourg (1857–1939), a Titus and Chase descendant who preserved a large collection of family manuscripts and compiled notebooks of photographs and recollections of early buildings in the Titusville area.

Others have also been generous. Alice E. Morrison of Cooperstown kindly lent her files of information about Titusville buildings and answered questions about people and places. Information about individual architects was provided by Craig Bobby of Lakewood, Ohio; Daniel D. Reiff of Fredonia, New York; and Pauline J. Kelton of Niles, Michigan. Additional historical information was provided by David L. Weber of Pleasantville, Annette L. Lynch of Meadville, and Dennis L. Armstrong of Franklin. Adam Sparks of Oil City provided photographic expertise, and Charles M. Herrold Jr. of Pittsburgh gave general support.

INTRODUCTION

In 1859, in Venango County near a spring that oozed petroleum into a small stream called Oil Creek, Col. Edwin L. Drake drilled the world's first successful oil well, touching off a stampede that resembled the California Gold Rush. The small village of Titusville, located about a mile north, in Crawford County, grew into a city of 10,000 by 1870, and it is still a city of 6,000 today. Oil City, 20 miles to the south, at the junction of Oil Creek and the Allegheny River, grew almost as rapidly, and other towns sprang up in the valley in between, wherever oil was discovered. One of these, about halfway between Titusville and Oil City, was consequently named Petroleum Center and boasted a population of 10,000 by 1868, although abandoned in the late 1870s when neighborhood wells ran dry. A third city had an even shorter career: Pithole, located on a small tributary of Oil Creek, about seven miles east of Petroleum Center, was founded in 1865, reached 15,000 inhabitants in 1866, and was almost completely abandoned by 1868.

The influx of people and money caused an unprecedented wave of building, which this survey explores.

During this period, some buildings were designed by architects rather than by contractors. Those working in Titusville included:

Emmett E. Bailey (1872–1942) initially partnered with Frank L. Charles, later becoming a sole practitioner in Oil City. His Titusville houses were neo-Colonial, but he designed additions to the Jefferson and Venango county courthouses that matched their Italianate details.

Joseph M. Blackburn (1813–1891) a Yorkshireman, spent his career in Cleveland, Ohio. Responsible for many buildings there, he also designed the First Presbyterian Church of Youngstown, 1866–1868; the Chester Bullock and Gideon Mosier residences in Meadville, 1868; and the James A. Garfield residence in Mentor, Ohio, in 1880. His Titusville works were mainly grand projects in the mansard style.

Charles Brigham (1841–1925) a prominent Boston architect, designed the Massachusetts State House extension and First Church of Christ, Scientist, there, as well as eight buildings for Henry H. Rogers in Fairhaven, Massachusetts, Rogers's birthplace.

John Sweeney Coddington (1824–1894), born in Geneva, New York, called himself a builder as well as an architect. He worked in Edinboro, then in Meadville, where he made an unsuccessful proposal for the Crawford County Court House and designed the David V. Derickson residence in 1867. He later made his home in Mentor, Ohio, where he died.

Enoch A. Curtis (1836–1907) a native of Busti, New York, was a trained architect with the longest connection to Titusville, and his work spanned the Second Empire to the Richardson Romanesque and Queen Anne styles. Although he lived in Fredonia, New York, he maintained a Titusville office in the 1870s and was responsible for the Elm Street School and the Warren and Venango Railroad Depot as well as the buildings illustrated in the text. He worked in the oil region through the 1890s. In Emlenton, he was responsible for the Presbyterian church, Union School, Bennet Opera House, and J. C. Porterfield residence. In Pleasantville, he designed the Holeman Opera House and remodeled the S. R. Brown block, and in Bradford, the Oil Exchange/Odd Fellows Building. Oil City had a number of his buildings: the National Transit Company, Grace Methodist and Christ Episcopal Churches, the Benjamin Brundred residence, and the City Hospital.

Dr. Charles B. Hammond (born about 1817 in New York), listed as an architect in 1870, also appeared as a physician, dentist, and real estate agent.

Philip M. Hesch Sr., (about 1831 to about 1915) was a Bavarian, working as a builder and architect in Titusville by 1870, then moved to Santa Fe, New Mexico, in 1882, where he died.

Philip M. Hesch Jr. (1854–1915) worked with his father as a builder and graduated from the University of Pennsylvania's School of Architecture in 1879. He spent 1882 to 1889 in New Mexico and then went to Magnolia, Mississippi. Opening an office in Titusville in 1893, he spent the rest of his life there, except for 1903–1904, and designed the Odd Fellows' building and St. Walburga's Church, besides the buildings noted in the text. He produced somewhat restless Queen Anne designs.

John F. Jackson (1867–1948) practiced in New York City, with Edwin J. Rosencrans as Jackson, Rosencrans and Canfield, then Jackson and Rosencrans from 1901 to at least 1915, when he opened his own office. He specialized in neoclassical railroad stations and urban YMCAs and was responsible for many buildings in Passaic, New Jersey, the Bensons' hometown, including the Reid Memorial Library in 1902 and the Byron D. Benson II residence.

W. W. Johnson may have been the man of that name who designed the G. H. Bartlett house in Buffalo, New York, in 1896.

James Melcher may have been the "Bourse" Melcher who appeared as a contractor and builder in the 1865 Titusville business directory.

Edwin L. Pitcher was listed as an architect in 1870 but appeared in the 1872 city directory as an oil producer.

Hiram Smith (born about 1814) was a New Yorker and worked as a carpenter in Chautauqua County for at least 20 years before relocating to Titusville, where his name is connected with some of the most lavish Second Empire–style homes. His property was sold by the sheriff in 1874, and he was living with his son near Bradford in 1880.

Marcus Smith, born in Connecticut about 1812, was a carpenter in Painesville, Ohio, arriving in Titusville before 1870, and disappearing by 1880.

George S. Stewart (1825–1898) born in Conneaut Lake, Pennsylvania, became a carpenter and builder and settled in Titusville about 1863. He superintended the construction of the Petroleum Bank and considered the Chase and Stewart Block his most significant work. He died in Bradford.

A. M. Tarbell was listed as an architect and builder in 1870, but was not a close relative of Franklin Tarbell. He may have been Andrew M. Tarbell (1806–1878), who was a carpenter in Erie in 1866.

Charles W. Terry (1849–1931) worked in Oil City, 1888–1904, then returned to Wichita, Kansas, and died in Alhambra, California. His Titusville work used the Queen Anne vocabulary.

William VanUlrich (or simply Ulrich), a civil engineer, and reputedly the nephew of the commandant of Strasbourg, came to Titusville from Erie in 1870. His Titusville buildings were rather florid Second Empire designs, as was his Grandin Block in Tidioute.

William M. Vaughn was listed as an architect in 1870 and as a carpenter in 1871.

William Webster was born in England about 1831, arrived in Titusville about 1870, and moved to Rochester, New York, in 1875.

Alexander Woodward (1832–1910) was an Irishman who worked as both architect and builder. He moved to Kansas City, Missouri, by 1890, where he died.

Henry E. Wrigley (1840–1883) was a civil engineer as well as an architect. He married Sallie Abbott, the daughter of an oil tycoon, which may have gained him commissions.

One

TITUSVILLE PRECURSORS

For the first several decades after the settlement in Titusville by Jonathan Titus and Samuel Kerr in 1796, most structures were built of logs. After sawn lumber became available, weatherboarded log and then frame buildings were constructed. Early examples, and modest later ones, had few details to identify them with any style. Titus's home, at 110 Arch Street, featured mantels carved by a man named Cowan in the 1814 log wing, and the 1823 addition was frame. Still, it faced a dusty commons stretching north to Spring Street, which Titus used for farm storage. He laid out a town, which he called Edinburgh, in 1816 and established the grid pattern of streets. Lots sold slowly, and Titusville only had about 150 inhabitants before Col. Edwin L. Drake's discovery. Titus's son-in-law Joseph L. Chase owned much of the land north of Spring Street and west of Franklin Street, and his home, office, and garden occupied the block between Spring Street and Pine Street (soon renamed Central Avenue). His brother Edward H. Chase, another Titus son-in-law, owned a corresponding tract east of Franklin Street. Merchants and offices strung along the south side of West Spring Street, and homes were widely scattered.

Even in a small town, homeowners were conscious of existing fashions, and soon Greek details appeared on buildings. The larger buildings in the Greek Revival style (1820–1860) often had porticoes with round columns, copied from their ancient Greek prototypes, and smaller buildings featured flat pilasters attached directly to the walls, but both were topped with heavy cornices and pediments.

Local carpenters followed pattern books for stylish details, which they applied to projects at hand. The Cherrytree Presbyterian Church, built about 1838, was extremely plain, except for the elliptical arched triple window, which resembled the doorway of the Chase Mill house. The Cherrytree Academy, of the same period, had corner pilasters and a deep modillioned cornice, a much more decorated building. These similar elements probably came from the same source, whether the mind of the builder or from the pattern book he copied.

Nos. 111–113 West Spring Street. While there is no known photograph of Jonathan Titus's house, it may have resembled the James Brawley residence, built on Spring Street perhaps as early as the 1820s and moved to 222 East Central Avenue about 1865. It was very plain, with no ornamentation except the front doorway, which had sidelights and a classical frame, implying heavy stone elements. The left third and large windows are later additions. (Drake Well Museum.)

No. 102 Union Street, Presbyterian Church. The first frame church belonging to the Titusville Presbyterian congregation was built from 1833 to 1837, at a cost of $1,500. It was plain on the outside, with a gable facing the front. Inside, between the front doors was a raised semicircular pulpit, reached by four steps, behind a railed platform where the church elders sat and the communion table was located. (Drake Well Museum.)

No. 732 East Main Street.
James Parker probably built his home after buying the property in 1854, and it shows more advanced Greek Revival detailing: a plain but heavy cornice under the eaves and over the door and window frames. The front door has sidelights and a transom, in an elaborate frame. The house was moved to its current location in 1868, when Jonathan Watson built his mansion on its former site. (Drake Well Museum.)

Chase Mill House. Joseph L. Chase and Thomas H. Sill established mills east of Titusville about 1835 and built this house as a residence for Charles L. Chase, the superintendent. The lot was landscaped, with a cut-stone retaining wall at the roadside and entrance steps rising in the middle. Although not a large house, it is quite formal, with the pilasters at the corners and the elaborate cornice.

No. 302 West Spring Street. This house, built in 1849 by Dr. John Shugert, was in the form of a central two-story block flanked by one-story wings. Its heavy Greek Revival cornice was plain, but the Greek porticoes, with Doric columns, dress up the design. The lightweight gallery on top of the central portico, however, suggests the Federal style. (Drake Well Museum.)

No. 624 West Spring Street. The original builder of this house is unknown, but Elizabeth Hequembourg dated it from about 1860. It is also Greek Revival, but with only one side wing. Generally simpler in design than the Shugert house, its cornices are lighter and it lacks the Doric porticos, having a side porch with square posts. (Drake Well Museum.)

No. 125 West Main Street, First Building. The first Titusville school was built in 1859 and burned in January 1866. This view shows the back, so one cannot tell how the belfry was integrated into the front facade. The building had a wide, Greek Revival cornice and narrow pilasters at the corners. It lacks the usual symmetry of the style, but the east wing may be the one added in 1863. (Drake Well Museum.)

No. 226 East Main Street, Hampson House. Built by Rev. George W. Hampson about 1840, the house was more famous as the Titusville home of the Edwin L. Drake family. It was very plain with a simple Greek Revival doorway. It was moved to 323 North Kerr Street to make way for the Sterrett House in 1870 and was demolished in 1956. (Drake Well Museum.)

13

NO. 203 EAST MAIN STREET. This house, built about 1865 by ironworks owner John C. Bryan, has a Greek Revival pediment on the front, with heavy cornices and two-story pilasters at the corners. The arch-topped windows and the octagonal bay are of the newer, Italianate style. The front porch is not original. Celia McMullen, Bryan's mother-in-law, lived next door, and both moved farther east on Main Street in 1870. (Drake Well Museum.)

NO. 321 NORTH FRANKLIN STREET. Samuel S. Fertig, an oil producer, built this town house about 1865. Unlike some of the more pretentious homes, the gables do not face the street, and the only decorative element is the arched frame of the front door. (Drake Well Museum.)

Two

TITUSVILLE RESIDENCES FROM 1860 TO 1880

With the prosperity of the oil boom, homes became larger and more elegant. Numbers of new buildings began to rise in 1865, and construction reached a peak in 1870 and 1871, declining with an oil price slump in 1872 and a national depression that began in 1873. With very few exceptions, the buildings from this period were either Italianate or Second Empire in style, but the amount of detail on buildings varied considerably.

Large residences appeared, often with stables, outbuildings, and even fenced parks and greenhouses. In the late 1870s, real estate prices and construction costs dropped, as the centers of oil production moved farther away from Titusville, and some houses sold for less than it cost to build them.

The period witnessed several very popular styles of buildings. The Gothic Revival or cottage style (1840–1860) produced few buildings that were literal copies of Gothic originals; most used Gothic ornament on buildings of modern shape.

The Italianate style (1840–1875) evoked villas in Italy. The closest copies featured many of the details that the Italians had developed for coolness in their warm climate: high-ceilinged rooms lighted by pairs of tall narrow windows, flat roofs with wide overhanging cornices supported by large brackets, balconies shaded by canopies, and wide verandas around the house. Smaller versions only copied details. Irregularity in plan was also sought for picturesque effect: projecting wings, octagonal bays, and general asymmetry were preferred to plain, rectangular buildings.

Second Empire style (1860–1890) was inspired by rebuilding in Paris beginning in the 1850s, and its primary identifying feature was the mansard roof. Named after the 17th-century French architect, François Mansart, a mansard roof was usually at least one story in height, with very steep sides punctuated by dormer windows. Irregular plans continued to be popular, and many American Second Empire designs were nothing more than Italianate ones with mansard roofs placed on top. The mansard became something of a status symbol, and even very modest houses were dressed up with them.

No. 107 North Franklin Street. Nelson Kingsland built this home with its two-story Ionic portico between 1862 and 1864, the last of the Greek Revival houses in Titusville. Kingsland sold his home and business in 1864 and returned to Keeseville, New York, to operate a foundry and nail factory. The house was converted into the Bush House hotel and then became Titusville City Hall in 1872. (Drake Well Museum.)

No. 213 North Perry Street. This house, in the Gothic Revival or cottage style, has the same form as many Greek Revival examples—a pedimented central block flanked by lower wings, but instead of wide temple cornices, the eaves are decorated by sawn wooden scrollwork. Built by Charles V. Culver and described as a "frame cottage dwelling house," it was sold by the sheriff in 1866. (Drake Well Museum.)

NO. 413 WEST SPRING STREET. This house, built by nitroglycerine manufacturer James R. Barber around 1866, added more Gothic elements: wood scrollwork window caps and the round attic window. The vertical board-and-batten siding suggests the lines of Gothic architecture, although it was also used on Italianate buildings at this same time. (Drake Well Museum.)

NO. 314 EAST MAIN STREET, STAGE ONE. This house is plain, but its nonclassical stoop and steep central gable qualify it as a Gothic cottage. It was built in 1864 by Justin Pomeroy, proprietor of the Pomeroy House, and he sold it the next year. The early date of this photograph is supported by the heavy wooden fence, as protections against roaming animals were no longer needed by the 1870s. (Drake Well Museum.)

MAIN STREET. The house in this photograph, labeled "Burgess House, Main Street 1865," has not been identified. With its jerkin head roofs, and the pointed arches on the front door frame and veranda, it is cottage Gothic in style. The large porch and the French windows on the first floor made it a house of some pretension. Some suggest it stood at 309 West Main Street. (Drake Well Museum.)

NO. 609 NORTH PERRY STREET. Jacob A. Cadwallader, a lawyer, oilman, and refiner, built the right-hand portion of this house about 1870. It is an essay in authentic Gothic design and features a central gable with Gothic steepness and heavy bargeboards. The left-hand portion was added about 1900. It is sympathetic to the original part, with a second but lower gable in the general Queen Anne style popular at the time.

No. 410 East Walnut Street. The rectory of St. James Memorial Episcopal Church was built in 1868 at 212 North Franklin Street for $5,000. The American Episcopal church wholeheartedly embraced the Gothic Revival style, and the rectory was the most Gothic of all Titusville examples. It had board-and-batten siding, arched rather than lacy wooden scrollwork in its multiple gables, and it featured a genuine Gothic window with tracery in the center of the second floor. (Drake Well Museum.)

No. 230 East Main Street. This house was built about 1865 by real estate dealer George Custar. The brick walls and lacy cast-iron windowsills and caps mark this as a relatively expensive house, and the arched windows and wide eaves identify it as mildly Italianate in style, although it lacks any fancy brackets.

No. 714 East Main Street, Stage One. This mansion was built by millionaire oil producer Jonathan Watson in 1868. Its Italian features are the bracketed cornice and floor-length windows that open onto the veranda, decorated with fancy scrollwork. Watson had a landscaped suburban estate, with barns and a greenhouse. After his bankruptcy in 1878, new owners added gables and verandas onto both sides of the house, and by 1896, a porte cochere appeared on the southeast corner. (Drake Well Museum.)

No. 307 East Central Avenue. Druggist Martin A. and Lizzie Funk McDonald built this home in 1869 and lost it in a sheriff's sale five years later. This two-part composition, with a gabled main block and a side wing, has a cornice more elaborate than the Custar house, and its verandas have fancy arches. A rectangular bay accents the wing, and the large lot was surrounded by an ornamental iron fence. (Drake Well Museum.)

No. 118 West Main Street. Lumberman Jonathan H. Clement had built this house before hardware merchant Frederick W. Ames bought it in 1865. It is large but fairly plain, although ornamented with fancy front and side porches, the former with a parapet, and a bracketed cornice on the front wing. Sold at sheriff's sale in 1879, it was purchased by Ames's sister-in-law, who returned it to the family. It was demolished about 1904. (Drake Well Museum.)

No. 114 West Main Street. This modest house was built before 1864 by Caleb O. Childs, another Brewer, Watson, and Company partner. It has details so quiet that it could be Italianate rather than Second Empire. In 1873, the Benninghoffs bought it and, instead of raising the roof in the front when they wanted to enlarge it, they apparently added a taller wing at the rear and extended the porch across the front.

No. 223 North Brown Street.
The H. S. Bates house was built about 1871 by a local builder for his own family. Although the house itself is quite plain, the door and window frames and the vestigial corner pilasters are ornamented with lacy wooden scrollwork.

No. 217 West Walnut Street. The Charles Church house was built in 1870 and designed by architect/builder Alexander Woodward. There is a front gable in the main portion, and the facade has a projecting bay window and a porch with exuberant scrollwork rising from the tops of the columns up to the eaves.

No. 409 North Perry Street. Joseph A. Scott, an oil dealer and refiner, apparently built this house about 1870 and lost it in a sheriff's sale in 1876. It is the traditional five-bay house with a central door, but on the second floor the central window is higher and topped by lacy scrollwork, and it in turn is surrounded by a gable with even more scrollwork. Octagonal bays flank the front door, and a continuous cornice connects them to the central porch.

No. 518 North Perry Street, Stage One. This home, built for Delos O. Wickham, a hardware merchant, in 1870, was designed by Hiram Smith. The projecting central gable with its steep roof could suggest Gothic Revival, although the double round-arched windows on the second floor make it Italianate. It was Colonialized about 1900 (see page 65). (Drake Well Museum.)

NO. 430 ROBERTS STREET. The Rexford Pierce house on the south side is one of several with a high flat facade, deep scrolled cornice, and large two-story bays. Built in 1870, it is situated on a large lot and originally had its own barn. An almost mirror image was built at 124 East Main Street by 1872. Pierce was a partner in Brewer, Watson, and Company.

NO. 315 NORTH DRAKE STREET. William D. Coldren built this house in 1870 for $6,000, and Marcus Smith was architect and builder. Similar to the preceding, it has a heavier cornice with larger brackets and the windows have square Gothic caps. The flush wood siding suggests masonry. Joseph J. Holden built a nearly identical home next door at 311 North Drake Street.

NO. 501 NORTH PERRY STREET. This house was built for wholesale grocer Edwin W. Granger in 1870 at a cost between $6,500 and $8,000. It has a shallow projecting bay toward the side street and its original porch. The main block has flush wooden siding and fancy arched wooden window frames, although lap siding is used on the rear wing. The Edward T. Hall house at 202 East Main Street is similar.

NO. 209 EAST MAIN STREET. The David Emery house (right) was built about 1871 when the Emerys moved to Titusville from Venango County. Taller than the preceding examples, it features a deeper cornice with fancier brackets and panels. The arched window frames are set off with lacy wooden scrollwork. The front porch was truncated in the 20th century. (Drake Well Museum.)

No. 320 West Walnut Street. The Francis H. Gibbs house is lower than the Emery house, but it is 40 feet by 52 feet and cost a substantial $12,000 when built in 1871. The flush wooden siding is scored to imitate ashlar stonework, an expensive refinement, and the corners are marked with slender colonnettes. There are hooded, arched wooden window frames with keystones, and the whole is topped with a dentiled cornice with elaborate scroll brackets. The house was sold by the sheriff in 1884. The large porch is probably 20th century.

No. 201 North Franklin Street, Cupola. Oil producer Ira Canfield built this large square brick house in 1865 and lost it in a sheriff's sale the next year. Its low arched windows have cast-iron caps used on many other buildings of the period, and the house is topped by a heavy dentiled cornice with robust brackets. The cupola on top has palladian windows on each side, its arched cornice supported by colossal double scrolls.

NO. 201 NORTH FRANKLIN STREET. This picture shows the house's original small stoop, with blocky, scrolled woodwork. While the main part of the house is only 28 feet by 33 feet, two large wings extend irregularly from the rear. It was said to be the first brick house built in Titusville. (Drake Well Museum.)

NO. 201 NORTH FRANKLIN STREET, PARLOR. This view of a parlor of the Canfield house was made about 1900, but it shows the very elaborately carved white marble mantel and its gilt overmantel mirror, both of which are probably original. The interiors were remodeled by Louis K. Hyde, who returned to Titusville to take charge of the family's Second National Bank in 1890 and added the large front porch at the same time. (Drake Well Museum.)

NO. 204 WEST MAIN STREET. Merchant and developer Joseph L. Chase built this substantial but relatively plain brick home in 1865. It was wider than the Canfield house and had a similar heavy cornice but a much simpler cupola. Instead of a stoop, the porch extended all the way across the front of the house. Chase had an entire block when his house was built, and he moved his frame office building there and maintained a small family cemetery on the lot as well. (Drake Well Museum.)

NO. 103 NORTH SECOND STREET. Edward A. L. Roberts built this brick house in 1868 and improved it in 1871. On a high stone foundation, the front porch spread across the front of the house. The windows were arched, the house had a fancy scrolled cornice, and the central cupola featured a cornice and balustrade. The small conservatory was an unusual feature. Roberts and his wife, Ida, separated, and he went to live in the Roberts Block in the 1870s. (Titusville, Pennsylvania, 1890.)

NO. 221 NORTH WASHINGTON STREET. Built around 1864, the Charles L. Maltby house is another large square house topped by a cupola, but it has the laciest decoration in Titusville. This shows its original appearance, with a high basement and wide front porch like the Roberts house. Its cupola was higher and topped with scrollwork around all four sides. (Drake Well Museum.)

NO. 221 NORTH WASHINGTON STREET, DETAIL. The Maltby window caps are wooden scrollwork resembling calligraphy. There is ornament on everything but the siding. The cornice is somewhat incongruously edged with Gothic tracery, but it is supported by brackets decorated by extremely lacy scrollwork. The house was radically remodeled by Josiah G. Benton in 1891, and in the 1920s, John H. Scheide added a brick and stone Tudor library in the rear.

NO. 332 NORTH WASHINGTON STREET. Oil producer Frederick Crocker built this house in 1870 for $15,000, and its bracketed cornice, centered by semicircular gables on the house and cupola, is one of the most elaborate in Titusville. The main block is square, with two octagonal bays on each side, and the porch formerly reached across the front. The windows have heavy wooden caps. Dr. Walter B. Roberts purchased this home in 1879. (Drake Well Museum.)

NO. 227 EAST CENTRAL AVENUE. Oil and lumberman George E. Brewer's house was unroofed by a tornado in 1860. He rebuilt and sold it to Jonathan Watson in 1862, the next year, Andrew B. Funk, a pioneer oil producer, bought it. Similar to the Chase, Maltby, and Roberts houses, its cupola was broader than some of the others and with a gallery. The house was huge, with the longest service wing in Titusville. The front portion survived at 111 South Drake Street and was demolished in the 20th century. (Drake Well Museum.)

NO. 215 WEST MAIN STREET, STAGE ONE. Oil producer and refiner William H. Abbott constructed this house in 1870 for the enormous sum of $40,000. His son-in-law Henry E. Wrigley was the architect. It was sold by the sheriff in 1874 but purchased by Abbott's brother-in-law, who allowed him to continue to occupy it. The semicircular bays, unique in Titusville, are probably not original, although they have window sashes like the others.

NO. 215 WEST MAIN STREET, STAGE ONE CUPOLA. This 1880s streetscape shows the original roof and cupola of the Abbott house at the upper right, with the tower of the Universalist church behind. This makes it appear that the Abbott residence resembled the Joseph L. Chase house across the street. The semicircular side bays do not appear, indicating they were later additions. (Drake Well Museum.)

No. 110 Arch Street. Jonathan Titus's daughter Olivia Moore inherited the homestead, which her husband remodeled about 1860 with Italianate details, including a low cupola and an unusual cast-iron porch. He soon gave in to financial pressures, selling the yard as building lots and converting his house into this hotel, adding a long rear wing. It burned in March 1866. (*Atlas of Oil Region,* 1865.)

Nos. 209–211 North Drake Street. This double house was apparently built by George Custar, perhaps as a stable, in the late 1860s behind his home on East Main Street. It appears to have always been a double house, with only four bays across the front. Its heavy cornice has ornate double scroll brackets, although it lacks the central cupola of the larger houses.

NO. 320 EAST MAIN STREET. Oil producer Sylvester H. Carpenter built this house in 1870–1871 at a cost of $6,000 to $8,000. William Vaughn was both architect and builder. The cornice is unusually heavy with large scroll brackets, and the porch has quirky scrollwork, which spans the intervals but also supports the cornice.

NO. 219 NORTH FRANKLIN STREET, ROBISON HOUSE. This is one of the better pictures of the William Robison residence, which was built by 1865 by a pre-oil Titusville resident. It was a plain square frame building, with a deep scrolled cornice, low Italianate roof, and a lacy porch across the front. It was demolished for the construction of the Titusville Women's Club. (Drake Well Museum.)

No. 401 North Washington Street. This simple frame house was built about 1865 by Alexander R. Williams, an oil producer and real estate developer. If the engraving of the house in the 1876 *Atlas of Crawford County* is correct, the walls have been raised and the attic windows inserted in the new cornice, as the old one ran directly across the tops of the second-floor windows.

No. 603 North Perry Street. This house, built in 1872 for oil producer and lumberman Charles H. Ames, has been remodeled so frequently its original appearance is conjectural. From the low slope of the roof and the wide bracketed cornice, it may have been a boxy Italianate house, like the Maltby residence. The Colonial porch was added in 1889, and further changes were made in the 20th century. (*Titusville, Pennsylvania, 1896.*)

No. 118 East Walnut Street. John S. Coddington designed this house for newspaper publisher William W. Bloss in 1870. The newspaper said it cost $5,000 and had a mansard roof, which it clearly does not. It does have expensive flush siding, with detailed arched window frames and a heavy cornice. Bloss ran an unsuccessful rival to the *Titusville Herald*, and the house was sold at sheriff's sale in 1874.

No. 120 East Main Street. Paul W. Garfield, an oil producer from Rochester, New York, built this house in 1871. Described as a "dwelling in French style," it cost $8,000 and had a tower in the center of the front, seen at the edge of this streetscape. The house, and a vacant lot to the west, were sold at sheriff's sale in January 1874. In the 20th century, it was radically remodeled. (Drake Well Museum.)

No. 602 East Main Street. Oil producer John Fertig built his towered Italian villa at the east end of Main Street in 1872. Damaged by fire early in 1873, it was promptly repaired. This 1896 view shows the tower was originally topped with wooden scrollwork, as was the smaller tower on the carriage barn. The original wraparound porch, with its scrolls and pendants, survives. (*Titusville, Pennsylvania, 1896.*)

No. 602 East Main Street, Detail. Finished with expensive flush wooden siding, the Fertig house has almost sculptural wooden arched window caps and some of the largest double scroll brackets in Titusville, even where the wing makes a shallow projection beyond the main wall.

NO. 324 EAST MAIN STREET. Oil producer Franklin Tarbell moved from Petroleum Center to Titusville and bought the Bonta House in Pithole for salvage. In 1870, he built this towered home for $8,000. The first-floor gallery in front of the French windows looks like the Bonta House's balcony railing, but the other recycled elements are harder to identify. His daughter, Ida, used the tower room as a study. (Drake Well Museum.)

NO. 324 EAST MAIN STREET, MAIN STAIRS. The main stairs of the Tarbell house curve up from the front hallway, with a wall niche partway up. Two parlors opened to the east of the hall. The top of the tower and the wing with the second parlor were removed in the 1920s, a new porch added to the front, and a higher roof with dormers placed on top.

No. 430 East Main Street. Celia McMullen built this house in 1870 for $13,000, with Hiram Smith as her architect. The front facade is symmetrical, with one set of double windows on either side of the central projection, which once sported a tower. Celia came from Warren in 1865 and bought a lot next to her son-in-law, John C. Bryan, who operated the Titusville ironworks. As her new house was going up, Bryan was building a brick mansion across Brown Street.

No. 604 West Walnut Street. Dr. George O. Moody apparently built this house about 1872 but soon lost it in mortgage foreclosure. Its tower is unusual since it rises from the center of the roof like a cupola, rather than along the front of the building. In the Italian manner, the porch encircled the front of the house and has an unusually detailed parapet with brackets and urns. (Drake Well Museum.)

No. 610 North Perry Street, Stage Two. This is another view of the John Eaton house, which appears on the cover. It shows a tower, which was either not visible in the other photograph or was added after 1873. Situated on a sloping lot between Perry and Union Streets, the home's terraced lawn provided an excellent view of the city. (*Atlas of Crawford County*, 1876.)

No. 310 East Main Street. Oil producer James H. Caldwell owned several of Titusville's mansions. He built this one, described as "an Italian villa with mansard roof," in 1870 at a cost of $10,000, with John S. Coddington as his architect. The walls are expensive ashlar-grooved flush wooden siding, and the cornice is heavily bracketed. The low mansard roof has an extreme flair, so that it almost looks jaunty.

No. 303 East Main Street. Lewis Hallock built this house in 1865, making it one of the earlier examples with mansard roofs. The roof has a pronounced curve, but aside from the large bay in the front, the house's original appearance is a mystery, since it has been Colonialized with a redbrick veneer.

No. 126 East Main Street. James R. Barber announced in 1871 that he built a "2 story dwelling with mansard roof," at a cost of $6,000. The plan resembles that of the house next door at 124 East Main Street, a three-bay front, with a large octagonal bay on the side, but it is topped with a mansard and arched dormer windows instead of an Italian flat roof. Even the original porch survives, although the columns are evidently replacements.

No. 413 North Washington Street. This house was one of Titusville's showplaces for 40 years, due to its gardens. There may have been an earlier house, as J. Theodore Briggs in 1865 paid $11,500 for the property. George K. Anderson, of Petroleum Center, paid $9,000 in 1868, and he apparently built this house the next year. Almost an entire half block was laid out as a garden with a pond and fountain. (Drake Well Museum.)

No. 413 North Washington Street, Garden Elevation. The Anderson mansard had a dual slope, in the French fashion, but the gables atop the dormers were unusual. The side porch was elaborate with scrollwork arches and a balustrade with corner urns and a central cartouche, but the other details are simple. The estate, sold by the sheriff in 1876, was purchased in 1878 for $20,000 by Edward O. Emerson, an oil and natural gas producer. (Drake Well Museum.)

No. 304 East Central Avenue. Maj. F. Benedict, an oil producer from Enterprise, built this house in 1870 for $22,000. Architect John S. Coddington produced a narrow design, with a bay at the end of a projecting wing and a three-story mansarded tower facing the main street. The mansard had a dual slope, like the Anderson house, but its dormers were so tiny as to be barely functional. (Drake Well Museum.)

No. 314 Union Street. Jairus H. Winsor began this house in 1871. Situated on a huge terraced lot overlooking the city, it was the grandest and one of the largest, originally 50 feet by 62 feet, and cost $20,000. Winsor went broke, and it sat empty until purchased in 1874 by oil producer James C. McKinney. Architect Enoch A. Curtis produced an irregular plan, its mansard taller and straighter than many and its tower substantial. McKinney and his daughter, Charlotte, stand on the lawn, and his sons, James and Louis, occupy the buggy at the lower left. (Drake Well Museum.)

NO. 314 UNION STREET, SOUTH SIDE. About 1900, McKinney added encircling verandas and removed the iron roof cresting. This view from the south shows the terraces cascading down the hill, with the original carriage barn behind the house and a new Queen Anne brick one on Union Street at the right, which stood until 1980. After 1900, a classical bow-fronted porch replaced the narrow one along the south side of the house.

NO. 314 UNION STREET, FRONT PORCH. Domenico Minoggi of Talamo's in Titusville frescoed the interior, and everything else came from Buffalo: the walnut woodwork, custom furniture, and bronze-mounted fireplaces were supplied by Weller, Brown and Messmer; Earbacker and Davis provided gas chandeliers; and Adam, Meldrum and Anderson provided the Brussels carpeting. This view shows the 1900 front porch. Empty, the house was demolished in 1939. (Drake Well Museum.)

No. 526 East Main Street. In 1870–1871, William P. Johnson, an oil producer from Rouseville, built the second most elegant home in Titusville at a cost of $28,000, with Hiram Smith as the architect. The house was brick, with arched stone window caps and keystones. The mansard was covered in a design of multicolored slate with iron cresting. When Johnson went bankrupt, the house was purchased by James Parshall in 1872. (Drake Well Museum.)

No. 557 Chestnut Street, Meadville. In 1868, architect Joseph M. Blackburn of Cleveland designed a brick mansion for Meadville merchant Gideon Mosier. It featured an unusual octagonal cupola atop a central pavilion with pediments and oval dormers. Blackburn also designed the Parshall Hotel and Opera House for James Parshall in 1870, so it hardly seems accidental that Hiram Smith's Johnson house included the same cupola and gables in the mansard roof. (*Meadville Saturday Night*, 1889.)

NO. 526 EAST MAIN STREET, PLAN. While Hiram Smith's exterior may not have been completely original, his interior plan was. From the front, it appeared the tower was in the center of the facade, but the east dining room wing was set back so that the pavilion with the cupola actually faced both streets at the corner.

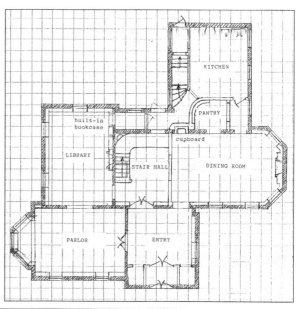

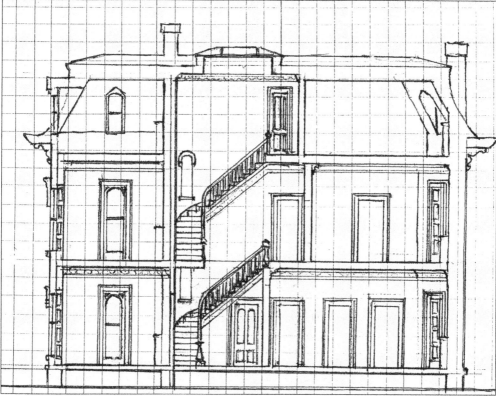

NO. 526 EAST MAIN STREET, CROSS SECTION. Rather than the customary central hallway, the Johnson house had a skylit three-story rotunda in the center of the house. On the ground floor, the parlor and dining room opened from it, and the stairs led up to the second-floor bedrooms and to a ballroom on the third floor. This cross-section runs east to west through the rotunda, facing north.

No. 526 East Main Street, Library Ceiling Rosette. The pedimented walnut overmantel mirror and built-in bookcases in the library had been removed shortly before photographs could be made in 1984 prior to demolition. The lower part of one section of the bookcases included a door into the rear hall. This plaster rosette was on the library ceiling. The plaster cornices in the main rooms were elaborate: cove moldings were filled with convex plaster filigree.

No. 504 East Main Street. Hiram Smith was also the architect of what was probably the third grandest home in Titusville, built for John C. Bryan in 1870–1871. The central tower entry led to the stair hall, flanked by rooms on either side of the front facade. A projecting wing on the side probably included the dining room, and an arcaded veranda wrapped around the corner, its base enclosed in intricate wooden filigree. (Drake Well Museum.)

No. 504 East Main Street, Mantelpiece.
The Bryan house cost $40,000 to build with cast-iron caps on the arched windows, an elaborate cornice with scrolls, patterns in the slate mansard roof, iron roof cresting, and a mansarded tower. The whole was surrounded by a cast-iron fence in a geometric pattern, with stylized spikes on the top. Inside, fancy marble mantels like this one were used even on the second floor.

No. 504 East Main Street, Stage Two. Reverses forced Bryan in 1872 to sell his home; oil man Daniel H. Cady and Standard Oil executive John D. Archbold owned it before it was purchased in 1884 by haberdasher turned oilman and civic leader John J. Carter. He added an encircling veranda and built a large greenhouse to the east of the house. (Drake Well Museum.)

No. 420 East Main Street. In 1871, oil producer William H. Wood built this two-story brick mansion, with an octagonal bay on the west side, for $15,000. It features cast-iron caps over the arched windows, patterned slate on the mansard, which has molding along the top and corners, and massive dormers with arched pediments. The original wooden front porch had a complicated design, including pendant drops in the arches between the columns. (Drake Well Museum.)

No. 1407 Elk Street, Franklin. The Samuel F. Dale house, in Franklin, with its heavy mansard roof, dormers, and large two-story bay, closely resembles the Wood house, although the windows are in pairs instead of single. It was built between 1873 and 1875 at a cost of $13,290. The resemblance is so close they either share a common prototype or one borrowed from the other.

NO. 226 EAST MAIN STREET, STERRETT HOUSE. Manufacturer William B. Sterrett married oil heiress Sadie Farel in 1871 and built this mansion the same year. Hiram Smith was the architect, and it cost $16,000. It had patterned slate and roof cresting, fancy cast-iron window caps, and deep-bracketed and dentiled cornice, as well as French-inspired oval dormer windows and a large finial on the tower. The porches were replaced in the 20th century.

NO. 226 EAST MAIN STREET, INTERIOR. This shows the interior of what may have been the reception room, with its mantel and overmantel mirror. Gibbs and Sterrett changed from making oil well machinery to farm equipment, and failed in 1884, but Sadie's independent means enabled her to keep her home.

No. 314 East Main Street, Stage Two. When oil producer Henry Byrom purchased the Justin Pomeroy cottage in 1870 for $7,000, he promptly spent another $4,000, replaced the roof with a mansard, and converted the central gable into a tower with its own mansard and diminutive dormer windows. By the time this picture was made about 1900, a new Colonial veranda had been added across the front. (Drake Well Museum.)

No. 314 East Main Street, Stage Three. A current photograph shows that the owners of the house continued to modernize it: the tower mansard was removed and the siding was covered with shingles to make it more like a bungalow. It is a far cry from its original Gothic cottage appearance on page 17.

NO. 507, 501 EAST CENTRAL AVENUE. In 1870–1871, James R. Jordan built the two-story brick home on the left for $3,000–$4,000, and Asa A. Bush built the house on the right for the same price. Both were modest; their top floors were plain mansards with rectangular dormers. The entry of the Jordan house had a tower with a curved mansard. The Bush house had a mansarded bay in the front and an entrance tower with a square dome. (Drake Well Museum.)

NO. 502 EAST WALNUT STREET. Hervey B. Porter, an oil refiner, built this house in 1871. The front wing, with nicely detailed bracketed and dentiled cornice, and wooden window caps, had a curved mansard with unusual arched double-windowed dormers and a large bay on the east side. A hyphen connected it with a large gabled rear wing. After a sheriff's sale in 1899, it received a new porch and small additions. It was razed in 2007.

NO. 214 WEST SPRUCE STREET. Lawyer Joseph A. Neill built this house about 1872. The pointed arches at the tops of the window frames and the wooden bracing in the gables make it a Gothic-style house, but the mansard on the central tower and the flush wooden siding confuse the issue. Sold at sheriff's sale in 1886, it was demolished early in the 20th century. (Drake Well Museum.)

NO. 322 NORTH PERRY STREET. Builder George S. Stewart in 1868 constructed five mansarded cottages for resale. They all had straight mansard roofs and rectangular dormers, but they were still considered very stylish and contained rooms for servants. All of the five have been modified over the years, and two were even attached to each other here.

NO. 227 EAST MAIN STREET, SCHUYLER HOUSE. A tall, rather straight mansard, punctuated by gables that pushed up into it through the cornice, is an unusual feature of this house, built by David Schuyler in 1870 for $6,000. It had wooden roof crests, tiny round dormers on the top level, and the very robust triangular porch that filled a corner between the two main wings. The house was demolished in 1896. (Drake Well Museum.)

NO. 708 NORTH PERRY STREET. The Chauncey F. Lufkin house was built in 1870 at a cost of between $15,000 and $20,000. A basic gabled house, it is dressed up with many features, including the entry tower with mansard roof and iron cresting. The dormer windows push up through the cornice here, forming complicated arches. The unusual dormer may have been a trademark of architect Henry E. Wrigley. The original front porch roof survives with new columns.

No. 417 West Spruce Street. A modest version of the Lufkin and Schuyler homes, the large octagonal bay and the shallow bracketed cornice make this house closer in design to the latter. The porch roof is probably original, although the base is not. The fenestration is unusually irregular. There is a similar house at 113 East Spruce Street.

No. 217 North Monroe Street. This house may have been built shortly after George J. Sherman purchased the lot in 1873. It is an ordinary three-bay, two-story, end-gabled house, but it is dressed up with a tower, topped by its own flamboyant gabled mansard roof.

NO. 503 WEST ELM STREET. This house, built by Clarence E. Safford in 1876, is one of the smallest mansard cottages. Even though small, it has all the French details: a full mansard, irregular plan, octagonal bays, a corner veranda, and a small tower, with its own mansard topped by iron cresting.

NO. 117 EAST WALNUT STREET. Roger Sherman, a prominent lawyer, owned this Italianate home when an engraving of it, without a tower, appeared in the 1876 Crawford County Atlas. The tower was added shortly afterward, decorated with a stick-style band beneath the cornice and topped with an abrupt mansard. A similar tower appears on the Kane residence at 506 West Walnut Street. (Drake Well Museum.)

NO. 402 WEST MAIN STREET. Tannery owner Samuel G. Maxwell added this mansarded tower behind an elaborate two-story porch to the Edward H. Chase homestead after he bought it in 1895. The tower has the last form of a mansard—a plain, straight roof with very little ornament. The rest of the Maxwell addition is in the newer Queen Anne style. The property went through a sheriff's sale in 1912. (*Titusville, Pennsylvania, 1896.*)

NO. 610 NORTH PERRY STREET, STAGE THREE. Oil producer John L. McKinney, after purchasing the John Eaton house, enlarged it to the north and altered the tower, adding a squat, straight mansard roof. The original porches on the south side of the house were glassed in, and a new veranda was added along the west front. About 1900, McKinney Colonialized his porch with substantial white columns. The house was demolished after McKinney died in 1937. (*Art Work of Crawford County, 1894.*)

Three

TITUSVILLE RESIDENCES FROM 1880 TO 1910

Titusville lost its boomtown flavor by 1880, although it was still prosperous. Industry was located there, and the city boasted streets lined with large stores and banks. While fewer houses were built, there were still significant projects. Not all were new construction, as owners of fine houses in the late 19th century did not often abandon them to build new ones. They remodeled their homes in more current styles, often so thoroughly that it is hard to imagine the buildings' previous appearance, and sometimes this was done more than once to the same building.

There were many styles in fashion during this era. Colonial Revival style (1870–1920) was stimulated by the Philadelphia Centennial Exhibition of 1876, which reexposed Americans to Colonial buildings and to contemporary English architecture. Houses made use of Georgian detailing, although in larger and more elaborate form than would have been used in the 18th century, and pilasters, broken pediments, and columned porches were hallmarks.

Queen Anne style (1880–1900) is an eclectic manner that developed from 18th-century English precedents. Contrasting materials—stone, brick, and wood—were fashionable, and small-paned windows appeared in many sizes and shapes, often in compositions of two or more. Turrets and gables were applied for interest at roof level, and porches favored extremely elaborate posts and woodwork.

Richardson Romanesque (1870–1900) was named for Boston architect Henry H. Richardson, whose designs were so widely copied that almost every town had its examples. Prime indicators of the style were walls of heavy, rusticated brownstone or dark brick, wide Syrian arches, and small windows with heavy stone frames, giving buildings an almost fortresslike appearance.

Beaux-Arts classicism (1890–1920), a lighter classical style advocated by the French École des Beaux-Arts, was popular for public buildings, as a reaction to the heaviness of the Romanesque. Columns were ubiquitous, and detailing was often exuberant.

No. 214 West Main Street. After Joseph L. Chase died in 1879, the Chase holdings in the 200 block of West Main Street were broken up. In 1884, oilman William T. Scheide built this Queen Anne–style house. Basically a square box, it is enlivened by gables, projecting wings, window compositions, and siding patterns.

No. 214 West Main Street, Roof Detail. This view of the roof shows the almost playful detailing of the house. Above the level of the gables, the straight rise of the roof turns into a double curve before ending in this platform with lacy iron cresting. Scheide was a noted book collector, and his son John H. Scheide developed the collection into one of the best in the world, owning a Gutenberg Bible.

NO. 224 WEST MAIN STREET. The James P. Thomas house was built about 1890. In the Queen Anne style, the brick walls and dark woodwork make it somber and the high gables make it imposing. Wall texture is emphasized, with shingles, stained-glass windows, and inset panels on the bays and gables. Ida, widow of Thomas Chase and Edward Roberts, married James P. Thomas, an early employee of the Roberts Torpedo Company and the builder of this house. (*Titusville, Pennsylvania*, 1896.)

NO. 204 WEST MAIN STREET, STAGE TWO. When David McKelvy, a lumberman and oil producer, bought the plain Joseph L. Chase house, he decided to keep up with his neighbors and added irregular projecting bays and porches and raised the roof and added gables, making it into a Queen Anne masterwork. They occupied it in the summer of 1885. (*Titusville, Pennsylvania*, 1896.)

NO. 334 EAST MAIN STREET. John S. Palmer built this home in 1887, and interior photographs show that the Palmers displayed family portraits and a table and piano from the 1860s in the parlor. Nevertheless, the house was modern: it had a wide wallpaper border with round flowers of Japanese inspiration, an oak lattice archway, and a bay window with fashionable small panes. (Drake Well Museum.)

NO. 416 EAST MAIN STREET. Alton H. Newton built this Queen Anne house in 1891. The profuse wooden scrollwork, the many gables, the iron roof cresting, and the different window forms are hallmarks. This was appropriate for Newton, who made his fortune in the lumber industry. (Drake Well Museum.)

NOS. 330 AND 334 WEST MAIN STREET. Built in 1898 by Joseph Seep as a wedding gift to his daughter, Lillian Quinby, this house displays the variety of details that Queen Anne builders used. There are shapes, gables, and textures everywhere. Edgar Quinby was a doctor, so the corner lot was purchased, and in 1900 they built an attached office building. (Drake Well Museum.)

NO. 330 WEST MAIN STREET, DORMER. A dormer of the Quinby house incorporates fishscale shingles, curved corners, scrolled brackets, and a small-paned window sash into one composition.

NO. 330 WEST MAIN STREET, CORNER WINDOW. The Quinbys used a favorite Titusville device: a leaded-glass window curving around a corner, with panels adjacent. Curves in wood and masonry were expensive, so this showed financial stability as well as good taste. The Fertigs added one to their home at 602 East Main Street when they remodeled their stairwell, and the Nixon house at 209 West Spruce was built with one.

NO. 114 EAST MAIN STREET. A smaller house than Quinbys', this home was probably built between 1886 and 1900 by William O. DeLong. It features a gable identical to the one on the Quinby house, but on a smaller scale, and an attractive arcaded porch.

No. 714 East Main Street, Stage Four. Charles Burgess, owner of the steelworks, purchased the Watson mansion in 1896, and Colonialized it. He added a palladian window flanked by bays on the second floor and replaced the Italianate porch with a stylish Georgian one, which wrapped around the south side of the house through a pavilion at the corner. (Drake Well Museum.)

No. 318 West Main Street. Theodore W. Reuting, a druggist, built this home about 1894, and Philip M. Hesch Jr. was his architect. It is much busier than the Scheide house, with bracketed bays on both floors and the octagonal domed tower in the center of the front facade.

NO. 227 EAST MAIN STREET, PAYNE HOUSE. Calvin N. Payne had prospered as a Standard Oil executive and replaced an earlier house with this one in 1896, designed by Charles W. Terry of Oil City. Not as restless as the Reuting house, its original tile roof gave it a heavy appearance, accentuated by the very large gables and the porches supported by groups of columns. (Drake Well Museum.)

NO. 215 WEST MAIN STREET, STAGE TWO. When Robert McKelvy purchased the Abbott house across the street from his parents in 1903, he radically remodeled it in classical garb. The cupola was removed, the cornice replaced with a delicately dentiled one, and two large Ionic pilasters and a pediment were added to the front, behind a one-story bow-front porch

NO. 623 NORTH PERRY STREET. This very correct Tudor Revival home was built by Edward O. Emerson Jr. about 1907. While an original 17th-century house would have had leaded-glass windows instead of small square panes, this home could otherwise have appeared in the English countryside.

NO. 518 NORTH PERRY STREET, STAGE TWO. Another radical remodeling occurred about 10 years after oil producer William C. Warner purchased the Wickham house. The stair hall on the south side became a center hallway, a whole new wing was built beside it, a new high roof was added, the original north gable rose in height and was duplicated on the south side, and a two-story porch and Colonial dormer were added in the center.

No. 701 North Perry Street. This Colonial Revival home was built about 1907 for John L. Emerson, another son of E. O. Emerson Sr. Designed by architect Emmett E. Bailey and called Hillhurst, it offers a spectacular view of the city. The details of this home are inspired by Colonial Georgian buildings, but the monumental portico and main doorway composition under the second-story balcony are clearly 20th century.

No. 118 West Main Street. Millionaire lumberman Isaac L. Shank built this Colonial Revival home in 1906–1907. Charles and Bailey of Oil City were the architects, and the interior was supplied by the Joseph Horne Company of Pittsburgh. The Colonial detail of this house is more meticulous than that of the preceding examples, but its sheer size demonstrates that it is 20th century.

No. 304 West Main Street. The only Richardson Romanesque home built in Titusville was that of Joseph Seep, head of Standard Oil Company's National Transit division. Seep moved a house off the lot to construct this design by architect Enoch A. Curtis in 1891–1892. The mass of the stonework matched the heavy slate roof. (Drake Well Museum.)

No. 304 West Main Street, Front Porch. This view of the front of the Seep house shows it had considerable detailing; the double Syrian arches of the front porch and their narrow trim above were supported by stubby pilasters with foliate capitals. Planters line the porch rails and steps, set off by extensive street frontage. (Drake Well Museum.)

No. 304 West Main Street, Dining Room. The Seep dining room had the latest gas and electric light fixtures, and the windows, of clear and stained glass, had lightweight curtains. The mantelpiece and furniture appear to be dark oak, in keeping with the rest of the woodwork. Like many mansions, this one was too expensive to maintain and was demolished in 1937. (Drake Well Museum.)

No. 319 West Walnut Street. The most common accessory to a prosperous residence was a private stable. This sophisticated barn with two double mansard roofs, both with small gables and cupolas, was apparently built by Birdsall and Taylor in 1870 as part of a residential commission for L. S. French. With the siding, it is impossible to determine what the original walls looked like.

No. 518 North Perry Street, Stable. The Delos O. Wickham stable could be stick style with the details on the second-floor door, the lozenge-shaped ventilator, and the plain cupola, but the arched openings probably identify it as vaguely French, like the house. The garage door is a mid-20th-century addition.

No. 303 North Washington Street. The Samuel S. Fertig stable, a large cruciform building, is clearly stick style, with its bold patterns in the east gable. The stable retains its original siding, doors, and fenestration, as well as its lofty spired cupola.

No. 714 East Main Street, Barns. Jonathan Watson's 1868 barn was a large two-story frame building with two cupolas. Since his estate was on the outskirts of town, the barn was larger than it could have been in the city. (*Art Work of Crawford County*, 1894.)

No. 526 East Main Street, Stable. Mansions often had stables that matched them. The Johnson stables (right) were brick and sported a mansard roof, punctuated by gables, just like the main house. This view shows the side entrance of the stable as well. (*Atlas of Crawford County*, 1876.)

No. 332 North Washington Street, Stable, Front. Walter B. Roberts's stables were the largest in Titusville. The long brick block has a central entrance tower, which may have had a mansard roof of its own. The front and side walls had pairs of tall windows, now bricked in. The curved mansard, with dormers in the front and gables on the ends, is supported by a heavy cornice, formed with patterns in the brick.

No. 332 North Washington Street, Stable, Rear. The rear wall of the stables features a long row of arched windows, apparently above the horse stalls. The stables were not part of the original Crocker project in 1870 but were added by Roberts in 1879.

NO. 504 EAST MAIN STREET, STABLE. The John C. Bryan stables have been remodeled and used as a science building, but it is still evident there was a tall front block, with a spired tower, and a slightly lower rear block with arched doors and windows. Both had curved mansard roofs with patterned slate, and the rear had dormers and a gable lined with wooden scrollwork.

NO. 332 NORTH WASHINGTON STREET, FENCE. Most houses had fenced yards, not out of necessity but to make statements about the owners of the lots they surrounded. This stone wall, topped by a series of nickel-plated rods and ball finials, was probably added to the lot after Walter B. Roberts purchased it in 1879.

No. 304 EAST CENTRAL AVENUE,
FENCE. The massive wooden fence
around the Major F. Benedict house
echoed the curves of the house,
and the one at the Eaton house,
shown on the cover, had the same
spiky forms as the residence. The
wood rotted in the damp climate,
and both were replaced with
iron fences in the 1880s. (Drake
Well Museum.)

No. 431 NORTH WASHINGTON STREET, FENCE. This iron fence surrounded the Anderson/Emerson gardens. It consists primarily of iron rods with cast-iron decorations and posts. The entrances were probably rearranged when apartment buildings replaced the gardens in the 1920s.

NO. 201 NORTH FRANKLIN STREET, FENCE. This picture shows the original cast-iron fence that surrounded the house, possibly added by Charles Hyde when he purchased it in 1866. While many iron fences were made of iron rods, this one is cast to suggest ropes and balusters. (Drake Well Museum.)

NO. 314 UNION STREET, FENCE. When James C. McKinney remodeled the house in the 1890s, he added stone retaining walls with gateposts and named the house Terrace Place. Although the house was demolished in 1939, these gateposts and some of the iron gates remain in the encircling stone wall.

No. 314 Union Street, Hitching Post. Cast-iron hitching posts survive here and there along the streets, although this horse-headed example is one of the more elaborate.

North Perry Street. This cut-stone curbside mounting block is one of the few survivors of what must have been a numerous tribe.

No. 504 East Main Street, Horticulture Display. Conservatory owners displayed tropical plants on their lawns during the summer. The Andersons had a conservatory across the alley south of the main house as early as 1876, and Jonathan Watson had conservatories behind his house in 1868, although no photographs of them survive. John J. Carter built one after buying the John C. Bryan house in 1884, and this is his front yard. (Drake Well Museum.)

No. 431 North Washington Street, Garden Fountain. The fountain in the Anderson garden was a huge cast-iron affair, topped by a statue of Hebe. Storks around a lower bowl spouted water, and it cascaded to another bowl and into the pond. (Drake Well Museum.)

Four

TITUSVILLE NONRESIDENTIAL STRUCTURES

Titusville justly prided itself on the number of houses of worship built in the city. Most Christian congregations chose some form of Gothic for their churches, but there were Greek Revival, Italianate, and Richardson Romanesque examples as well. The two Jewish congregations both chose a rather exotic style to emphasize their Near Eastern roots.

Being a commercial center, Titusville had dozens of office buildings and stores. The custom of the time was for the ground level of most commercial buildings, even hotels, to be rented out as stores, with the other businesses located on the upper floors. Even huge buildings like the Parshall Hotel and Opera House and the Brunswick Hotel required their patrons to climb stairs to the second floor. Downtown blocks of Franklin, Spring, and Diamond Streets and Central Avenue were lined with two- and three-story commercial buildings. When downtown real estate was highly desirable, new buildings replaced old ones each generation. Redevelopment in the 1970s swept dozens of old buildings away. Whole blocks were cleared for the construction of the Drake Mall alone.

Examples of all the styles used for houses can be found in commercial buildings. While the mansard roof of the Second Empire style is scarce, there were examples, and others used Second Empire details. There were Greek Revival buildings from the earliest period, followed by Italianate, Gothic Revival, Queen Anne, and classical styles, although the Italianate and Second Empire predominate.

Last of all, Titusville's residents also needed final abodes. Both Woodlawn and St. Catharine's Cemetery were established during this period and carefully landscaped. The monuments there run the gamut from Gothic to classical to Egyptian Revival. The monuments in Titusville differ from those in towns of similar population by their size and detail. Clearly the captains of industry preferred large monuments to enshrine their memory.

No. 210 North Franklin Street. St. James' Memorial Episcopal Church was built in 1863–1864 at a cost of $20,000. The building is stone but modest in size, with narrow lancets and a tiny rose window, authentically Gothic in inspiration. The nave has an open beamed roof flanked by low aisles. The slate roof was later patterned with colored slate and pierced by large triangular gables containing stained glass. (Drake Well Museum.)

No. 210 North Franklin Street, Campanile. Oddly, the church was not built with a belfry, which was remedied in 1893 by this free-standing 100-foot wooden bell tower north of the church, donated by James C. McKinney. Designed by Philip M. Hesch Jr., its details were properly Gothic, although there is no Gothic precedent for such a structure. (*Titusville Evening Courier*, 1906.)

NO. 214 NORTH FRANKLIN STREET, FIRST BUILDING. The second home of the Titusville Presbyterian Church was frame and Italianate in style. Finished in 1865 at a cost $17,000, it had vertical board-and-batten siding, and its louvered belfry had round arched windows that extended into arched gables in the cornice. A large triple window faced the street, flanked by two entrances in their own small gabled pavilions. (Drake Well Museum.)

NO. 214 NORTH FRANKLIN STREET, FIRST BUILDING INTERIOR. The interior of the Presbyterian church was surprisingly ornate. The elaborate trompe l'oeil frescoing may have been part of the $3,000 of improvements made in 1870 and may be the work of Arthur Talamo, an Italian by birth, who frescoed many buildings locally and also sold paint and wallpaper. (Drake Well Museum.)

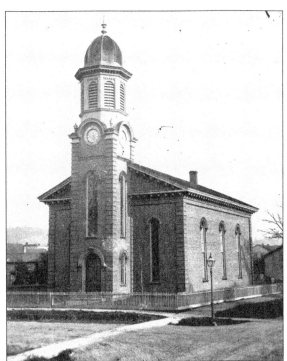

No. 221 West Main Street. The Universalist church is one of the most imposing. Built of brick in 1865, it features quoins on the corners of the building and tower and tall arched windows with cast-iron caps. The cornice is wide and bracketed, and a clock is mounted in arched gables at the top of the tower, although there was also an octagonal wooden domed belfry. The congregation dissolved in the early 20th century, and the church was sold. The architect was James Melcher. The church was sold at a sheriff's sale in 1880, was purchased by two church members, and finally sold in 1922. (Drake Well Museum.)

No. 105 North Perry Street. The Titusville Methodist Church was built in 1863. It was frame, 40 feet by 93 feet with board-and-batten siding, and its spire, which sprang from an octagonal drum, housed the first church bell in Titusville. The parsonage next door was built at the same time, but its little mansarded tower may have been a later addition. (Drake Well Museum.)

NO. 516 WEST SPRING STREET. St. Titus' Roman Catholic Church was completed in 1864. Built of brick, its arched windows were divided by mullions. The bell tower was topped by an octagonal structure of pilasters supporting low arches and crowned by a very shallow roof. A deeper chancel and transepts, designed by Philip M. Hesch Sr., were added in 1871, and the church was faced with stone and completely remodeled in 1935. (Drake Well Museum.)

NO. 516 WEST SPRING STREET, INTERIOR. The interior of St. Titus' church had elaborate trompe l'oeil frescoes. Only the large crosses on the walls and framed prints of the stations of the cross identify the church as Roman Catholic. After the enlargements of 1871, Arthur Talamo frescoed the walls, and a Derrick, Felgemacher and Company organ, 24 feet tall in a rosewood case, occupied the eastern transept. (Drake Well Museum.)

NO. 220 NORTH PERRY STREET. The Titusville Baptist Church, designed by James Melcher, was begun in 1865 and completed in 1868. Construction cost $25,000, and the building is Gothic in style with stone window sills, caps, and trim on its buttresses. The tower has lacy scrollwork below the bell tower and under its arched cornices above, and the spire itself has patterns in the slate. It suffered internal damage in a fire in December 1923. (Drake Well Museum.)

NO. 102 UNION STREET, GERMAN REFORMED CHURCH. The Titusville German Reformed Church was designed by Enoch A. Curtis and built in 1872. It resembles his Emlenton Presbyterian Church and includes a mansard roof in the tower, with vertical board-and-batten siding and pointed, Gothic windows. The spired buttresses on either side of the front are not structurally necessary but balance the composition. (Drake Well Museum.)

NO. 512 WEST MAIN STREET. Two St. Bridget's Academies burned in 1869, and a third was begun that fall. In 1870, the *Titusville Herald* called it St. Joseph's Academy and said it was being built at a cost of $14,000, with Philip Hesch as architect. Later it said the building under construction was only a connecting link between the two wings, each 35 feet by 70 feet, and it would be 40 feet square, all of brick, and topped with a mansard roof and an 85-foot central dome. Confusingly, architect Enoch A. Curtis claimed design credit for "St. Mary's Convent Academy." (Drake Well Museum.)

NO. 512 WEST MAIN STREET, AN EARLIER VIEW. While an 1870 article characterized the building as in the "Italian style of architecture," it clearly was French in inspiration with the mansards. The dome on the right (central) portion was never built, but the wings were quite ornate, with mansard roofs and turrets. The wing occupied by the Sisters of Mercy featured an elaborate niche for a statue of the Virgin Mary. (Drake Well Museum.)

NO. 318 NORTH FRANKLIN STREET. The B'nai Zion synagogue was built in 1871, to a design of William VanUlrich. It was frame, 26 feet by 75 feet, three stories in height, and cost between $8,000 and $10,000. The arches suggested an Eastern or Byzantine influence. The two tablets of the law topped the center of the facade, between two arcaded corner turrets with onion domes. The German Reformed Jewish congregation had dwindled to 13 members by 1885, and the building was sold in 1928. (*Titusville, Pennsylvania,* 1896.)

NO. 218 NORTH MARTIN STREET. The B'nai Gemiluth Chesed synagogue was built by a largely Polish Orthodox congregation about 1873. It is 30 feet by 56 feet and of the same general design as the other synagogue, although much plainer, with the same corner turrets and plan. (Drake Well Museum.)

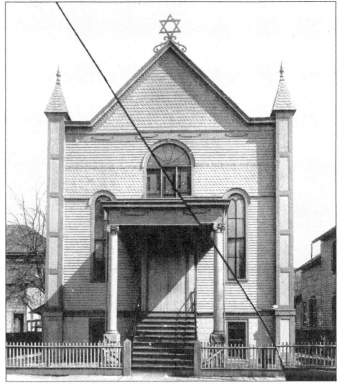

No. 214 North Franklin Street, Second Building. Enoch A. Curtis designed this Richardson Romanesque building for the Presbyterian Church in 1887. The sanctuary is T-shaped, with large stained-glass windows in each transept, a nave extending west from it between the tower, and an entrance porch. The roofed circular tower is unusual. (Drake Well Museum.)

The Emerson Chapel. The Emerson family built a chapel south of the church in 1906, in matching Romanesque style, with an entrance under a wide arch and flanked by narrow windows. On the south side, there is a shallow bay with tall arched windows. Originally it was a large hall, surrounded by broad balconies on three sides, but the interior has been gutted and reconfigured.

NOS. 128–132 WEST SPRING STREET, AMERICAN HOTEL. The 1864 American Hotel was a simple frame building, but it was enlivened by lacy wooden scrollwork above the windows. It incorporated the 1834 hotel built by the Robisons, was owned by Myer Kander, Jacob Strauss, and Joseph Stettheimer, and was operated by veteran hostler Maj. Samuel M. Mills from 1866 to 1868, until he went bankrupt. (Drake Well Museum.)

NOS. 134–136 WEST SPRING STREET, ORNATE STORE. The store building on the left, also built by Kander, Strauss, and Stettheimer in 1864, was almost baroque, with a huge round gable in its false front under an elaborate bracketed cornice, its second-floor windows topped by wooden scrollwork. (Drake Well Museum.)

Nos. 207–209 East Central Avenue. The Crittenden House hotel was built in 1865 by E. H. Crittenden, with an arched false front topped by giant wooden scrolls. Its heavy bracketed cornice placed it in the Italianate camp, and the canopied iron veranda on the second floor, above the wooden arcade on the first, is also in that style. The huge door at the lower left apparently led to the stables. (Drake Well Museum.)

Nos. 207–209 East Central Avenue, Side View. This side view of the Crittenden House (at rear) shows what a large building it was. Before the construction of the Soldiers' Orphan School, its pupils were housed here. The Crittendens lost their hotel, together with their public hall and liquor store buildings, at a sheriff's sale in 1866. (Drake Well Museum.)

NOS. 207–209 EAST CENTRAL AVENUE, INTERIOR. The hotel, purchased by William H. Abbott, was improved in 1870 and renamed the Abbott House. The billiard hall had skylights as well as gas chandeliers, and its walls were richly frescoed. With the proscenium arch and stage in the rear, this room could also have been used for theatricals. The hotel burned in 1872. (Drake Well Museum.)

NOS. 113–121 DIAMOND STREET. Crittenden Hall was a public hall on the second floor of this frame building, while the first floor was occupied by stores. It was built in 1862, after an earlier hall burned. The form is Italianate with a deep bracketed cornice and an arched doorway opening onto the second-floor balcony. After the Crittendens lost the building, the *Titusville Herald* occupied the second floor. (Drake Well Museum.)

NO. 114 SOUTH FRANKLIN STREET. The First National Bank building was the fanciest bank in Titusville. Built of brick by Charles V. Culver in 1864 and purchased by the bank for $21,500, it is five bays wide and the central windows with full arches, flanked by windows with low arches, are all capped with elaborate cast iron. The deep bracketed cornice, now removed, bounced over arched panels above the windows and was decorated with wooden scrollwork along the top and at the corners.

NOS. 102–106 SOUTH FRANKLIN STREET. This three-story brick store and office building was constructed about 1865 by Benjamin Waite, a wealthy hardware merchant from New Bedford, Massachusetts, and has fenestration similar to that of the First National Bank. It also has cast-iron window caps. Unlike the bank, its cornice was straight, supported by pairs of brackets. The building burned in 1933. (Drake Well Museum.)

Nos. 101–105 West Spring Street. The southwest corner of Franklin and Spring Streets was the site of Titusville's earliest store, opened by William Sheffield about 1816, and Zadock Martin had a hotel there until 1864. Charles V. Culver built this complex of 10 stores in 1863–1864 and sold the corner one, with a curved entrance wall, to his Petroleum Bank in 1865 for $20,000. (Drake Well Museum.)

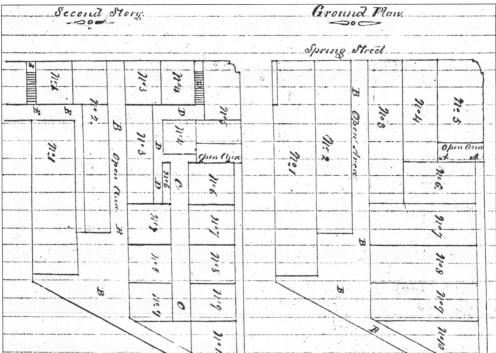

Nos. 101–109 West Spring Street, Plan. This diagram shows the layout of the 10 stores in Culver's complex, like a modern condominium, separated by open areas and sharing common hallways. The buildings were almost identical, with low arched windows with bracketed iron caps and a cornice supported by double brackets and topped by a low balustrade. (Crawford County Recorder of Deeds.)

No. 101 West Spring Street, Interior. After housing the Petroleum Bank, then the Titusville Savings Bank, which closed by 1874, and finally the Exchange Bank, which went into receivership in 1877, this building was purchased by E. O. Emerson, who used it for his office. He kept these wooden bank furnishings installed in the 1870s. (Drake Well Museum.)

Nos. 101–105 West Spring Street, Masonic Hall. In 1871, the Titusville Savings Bank made improvements to its corner at a cost of $7,000, and a Masonic hall was created by adding a third story at a cost of $6,000. The entire wall surface was covered by elaborate trompe l'oeil frescoes in a florid Gothic style, which transformed the room into a dark and mysterious place. (Drake Well Museum.)

NOS. 131–137 DIAMOND STREET. John Fertig owned a lot fronting on Diamond, Martin, and East Spring Streets and in 1870 built the three-story brick Fertig Block at a cost of $25,000, with Dr. Charles B. Hammond as architect. The walls were pierced with low arched windows, with stone sills but no caps, and the deep cornice had recessed panels between extremely large wooden brackets. (*Titusville, Pennsylvania, 1896.*)

NOS. 202–204 WEST SPRING STREET, STAGE ONE. The Second National Bank built this office about 1865. The windows on the second floor were the same as those on the First National Bank, although it lacked ground-floor storefronts and the frothy cornice of the former. The facade had an unusual flat-topped gable. (Drake Well Museum.)

NO. 311 NORTH FRANKLIN STREET. Sylvester Hill built his modest grocery store building in 1865 but used expensive sandstone for the walls. The ground floor has an arcade of three arches across the storefront, but the window frames on the second floor, the wooden cornice, and the low Italianate roof are plain.

NOS. 101–115 SOUTH FRANKLIN STREET. The Chase and Stewart Block (left), owned by Joseph L. Chase and George S. and Milton Stewart, was built in three parts. Architect George S. Stewart designed the three-story south end, built in 1870 at a cost of $24,000. The windows and cornice are both plain. The north end, housing the Odd Fellows hall, was built in 1870–1871 for the same cost. The central portion, with slightly different details and a fourth-floor mansard, was built about 1872. (Drake Well Museum.)

NO. 125 WEST MAIN STREET, SECOND BUILDING. The second Main Street School was a frame structure, in the form of a central gabled portion flanked by two slightly lower wings. Its belfry resembled that of the Presbyterian church, with arched openings under arched gables in the cornice. It was built in 1866, after its predecessor burned, and contained eight rooms. (Drake Well Museum.)

NO. 127 WEST SPRING STREET. The European Hotel was built in the late 1860s and then purchased in 1871 by the Roberts brothers, who spent $10,000 on improvements. The slightly arched windows have cast-iron window caps, like those used on the Custar house, which added detail to its otherwise plain facade. (*Titusville, Pennsylvania, 1896.*)

NO. 129 WEST SPRING STREET. Before purchasing the hotel, the Roberts brothers built their three-story brick bank next door in 1870, 22 feet by 90 feet, for $10,000. In 1871, they spent $5,500 for bank fittings inside. They copied the hotel cornice, making the two buildings appear one. However, the three stories of the bank contrasted with the four of the hotel; the ground floor had an arched stone arcade, and the very tall upper windows had stone caps with keystones. This view shows that the building also had fashionable scenic window screens. (*Atlas of Crawford County*, 1876.)

NO. 206 EAST CENTRAL AVENUE. The Bliss Opera House was an early performance venue, the high-ceilinged hall located above James A. Bliss's store. "Open every night," its patrons in 1865 were promised a "full stock company." The high arched windows announced its function, and the tall false front had a heavy cornice supported with paired brackets and a shallow elliptical gable in the center. Sold at sheriff's sale in 1866, it soon became a large furniture store. (Drake Well Museum.)

Nos. 111–113 West Spring Street. Corinthian Hall was the grandest of the early public halls, built of brick instead of wood and its extremely tall windows fronted by a stylish iron balcony. Built in 1865 by Jacob Strauss, Joseph Stettheimer, Gottlieb Frey, and Samuel M. Bear, all local merchants, it was sold by 1868 to Joseph Barnsdall, who made $1,000 of improvements to the building in 1871. It was sold at sheriff's sale in 1879, and by 1885, it had been renamed the Academy of Music.

Nos. 101–103 Diamond Street. With commercial real estate at a premium and the Crittenden Hall in decline, George K. Anderson in 1870 built his new Citizens Bank block on the small triangle of land in front of Crittenden Hall. Henry E. Wrigley was architect, and the building cost a substantial $20,000. The red brick, set off with bands of stone arching over the doors and windows, could be called Ruskinian Gothic, but the deep wooden cornice, with its elegant double classical scrolls, suggests the Italianate style. (Drake Well Museum.)

NOS. 201–207 WEST SPRING STREET. Oilman James Parshall built the Parshall Hotel and Opera House. Designed by Cleveland architect Joseph M. Blackburn, it was 125 feet by 110 feet and cost $140,000 in 1870; and a $35,000 addition, 68 feet by 85 feet, was added along Washington Street in 1871. Italianate in style, there were tall pairs of arched windows on the three floors above the storefronts, divided by quoins and topped by a deep bracketed cornice. The main and ladies' entrances, a ladies' parlor, and a 23-foot-by-52-foot bar and billiard room were on the first floor. (*Atlas of Crawford County*, 1876.)

NOS. 201–207 WEST SPRING STREET, OPERA HOUSE SIDE. In the western half of the building, Parshall's opera hall was 51 feet by 65 feet, and 36 feet high to the 16-foot skylit dome with a parquet, dress circle, two galleries, and four private boxes. Romeo Berea frescoed figures of Music, Comedy, Tragedy, and Poetry in the dome; the U.S. shield under a bust of King Lear, in front of figures of Music and Love, over the proscenium arch; and faux damask on the walls and galleries, all set off with gilt moldings, eagles, and cupids. (Drake Well Museum.)

NOS. 201–207 WEST SPRING STREET, DINING ROOM. The 23-foot-by-52-foot Parshall Hotel dining room was decorated for a banquet of the Titusville Commercial Club on May 24, 1871, but the room itself was surprisingly plain. The walls were not frescoed, and the window frames were a simple molding. Service was from kitchens below, staffed by three French chefs. There were 3 parlors and 18 suites, 10 with fireplaces, on the second floor, and all rooms had marble washstands with running hot and cold water. (Drake Well Museum.)

NOS. 201–207 WEST SPRING STREET, RUINS. The opera house opened on December 19, 1870, and the hotel the next spring, but their career was short. The block was totally destroyed in a spectacular fire on April 14, 1882. Volunteer fire companies fought each other for the honor of fighting the blaze, inspiring the city to establish its paid fire department. The foundations of the hotel, filled with rubble and surrounded by a high board fence, remained as late as 1890. James Parshall was ruined, and the property was sold at sheriff's sale in 1884. (Drake Well Museum.)

NOS. 209–215 WEST SPRING STREET, STAGE TWO. The Roberts Block at first was an elegant cooperative apartment building. It was 61 feet by 110 feet, four floors high plus a tall fifth-floor mansard, and cost $75,000. The Roberts brothers began construction in the fall of 1871, but the unfinished building collapsed onto the frame building next door in December. The brothers bought that lot and rebuilt at a cost of $100,000 the next year, adding a three-story wing at 215 West Spring Street, where the frame building had stood. (Drake Well Museum.)

NOS. 209–215 WEST SPRING STREET, STAGE THREE. The Roberts brothers' heads graced keystones in the center of the arcade across the storefronts. The tall arched windows above had stone sills and caps with keystones and were flanked by unusual slender colonnettes. As rebuilt by Enoch A. Curtis, the building was reinforced by brick cross walls and iron bolts through each floor so the walls remained standing even though the building was gutted when the Parshall block burned in 1882. Walter B. Roberts rebuilt again, substituting a fifth floor for the mansard. (*Titusville, Pennsylvania*, 1896.)

NOS. 209–215 WEST SPRING STREET, DINING ROOM. After the death of Edward A. L. Roberts in 1881, the building was converted into a hotel, and after the 1882 rebuilding, it was christened the Brunswick Hotel. It was renovated inside again in 1897 shortly before it was sold by Erastus T. Roberts, the doctor's son. This photograph shows the dining room, with pelmets at the windows, and wall panels outlined with faux bamboo. (Drake Well Museum.)

NOS. 209–215 WEST SPRING STREET, HALLWAY. This view of the circular light well in the upper lobby shows how imposing the Brunswick was. It was deemed the most lavish hotel in Crawford County at the dawn of the 20th century and was respectable enough to be the visitor center for the 75th anniversary of oil in 1934, shortly before its demolition. (*Titusville Evening Courier*, 1906.)

NO. 308 EAST WALNUT STREET. The Drake Street School, designed by architect William VanUlrich, was built in 1870 at a cost of $35,000. It had eight rooms and was decorated with all the devices of the Second Empire style: tall arched windows with fancy cast-iron caps set in brick walls bordered with quoins and topped with a mansard roof with dormers and an almost aggressive pattern in the slate. The central front tower had a square dome, also with patterned slate. (Drake Well Museum.)

NOS. 202–204 WEST SPRING STREET, STAGE TWO. The Second National Bank hired Joseph M. Blackburn to enlarge its building in 1871, and this unusual three-story stone Gothic building, with classical quoins and a mansard, was built in front and on top of the 1865 building. The rounded corner echoes that of the Petroleum Bank building, and the pointed arch window frames, particularly the triple ones, echo those of Blackburn's 1868 Mosier house. Original plans called for a marble front, but sandstone was substituted. (Drake Well Museum.)

Nos. 116–118 Diamond Street.
This building was apparently built in the early 1870s by Joseph and Philip Hoenig and designed by Enoch A. Curtis. Its cast-iron detailing is bold and heavy: the cornices above the storefronts and at the top of the facade and the window caps, particularly the central ones. The front of the building is not flat, but recessed panels flank the center bay.

Nos. 210–214 South Franklin Street. South Franklin Street was a mixture of small and large buildings. The tripartite three-story brick building on the left was the most imposing. Probably built in the early 1870s, it has panels of windows above the storefronts, and the cornice of the center set it apart from the two sides ones, the southerly of which housed the *Titusville Herald*. (Drake Well Museum.)

Nos. 109–113 East Spring Street. The Andrew S. Ralston block is conveniently dated 1872 in the central gable. Like the Hoenig block, an ornamented center bay was flanked by panels of windows. Ralston, an extremely successful oil producer, with assets of $130,000 in 1870, evidently decided to invest in real estate. (*Titusville, Pennsylvania, 1896.*)

Nos. 128–132 West Spring Street, Oil Exchange. The Titusville Oil Exchange in 1880 commissioned architect Enoch A. Curtis to design this Ruskinian Gothic building, its brick walls set with stone panels, bands, and arcades. The heavy cornice is topped with a low wooden parapet, which flanks a dormered tower. The front wing, 75 feet by 100 feet, contained offices, and a broad central corridor paved with encaustic tiles led to the exchange room in the rear, 40 feet by 60 feet and 45 feet high, with a gallery at one end. The exchange disbanded in 1897. (*Titusville, Pennsylvania, 1896.*)

NOS. 207–209 SOUTH WASHINGTON STREET. After the Parshall Opera House burned in 1882 and the Emery Opera House in 1887, a new theater building was needed. The Titusville Opera House was built in 1887 by Chauncy F. Lake but was a prompt failure, being sold at sheriff's sale in 1890. John J. Carter purchased it and resold it in 1904 to the Titusville Opera House Company. It was Queen Anne in inspiration, with arcades and a central neoclassical gable. The stage house is at right. (*Titusville Evening Courier*, 1906.)

NOS. 122–126 WEST SPRING STREET, REUTING BLOCK. Brick stores replaced the wooden ones on West Spring Street, and Enoch A. Curtis designed this Queen Anne block for druggist Theodore W. Reuting in 1890. The facade is enlivened by a shallow arch, flanked by fancy bays with multipaned windows above a recessed entry spanned by a grille. (Drake Well Museum.)

Nos. 142–148 West Spring Street. The Algrunix Block (named for its owners, Edward Allen, Samuel Grumbine, and Hattie Nixon) is a busy Queen Anne mix of details made Middle Eastern by the muezzinlike corner turret. It was built in 1894, and Philip M. Hesch Jr. was the architect. (Drake Well Museum.)

No. 213 North Franklin Street. In 1902, the Byron Benson family offered to build a city library in memory of their parents and to provide $2,000 annual funding. Titusville accepted the offer, and this classical building was constructed and opened in 1904. The redbrick walls are ornamented by shallow panels, as well as stone bands, window caps and keystones, and this Ionic portico. The architects were Jackson and Rosencrans of New York City. (Drake Well Museum.)

NO. 219 NORTH FRANKLIN STREET, WOMEN'S CLUB. This building, next to the Benson Memorial Library, was built for the Titusville Women's Club in 1904. It too is classical, with a white Ionic arcade topped by an enclosed loggia in the center of the front, between windows in redbrick arches. False windows flank a broad arch above the Ionic end portico. W. W. Johnson was the architect.

WOODLAWN CEMETERY GROUNDS. The original graveyard, on Brook Street, and the North West Cemetery, on West Spring Street, were both too small, so Jonathan Watson, R. D. Fletcher, and Edward H. Chase established Woodlawn Cemetery. In 1871, the grounds were laid out by William Webster of Rochester, New York. The stream in the central ravine became a pool for swans, with a fountain bordered by classical stone urns. (Drake Well Museum.)

ABBOTT PLOT, WOODLAWN
CEMETERY. William H. Abbott's was
one of three monuments supplied
in 1873 by the W. H. Fullerton
Company, of Factory Point, Vermont. A
substantial plain marble base supports a
life-sized statue of Hope.

ROBERTS PLOT, WOODLAWN CEMETERY. The Edward A. L. Roberts family plot was the most
elaborate in the cemetery, with a florid Gothic canopied central monument, sheltering a statue
of Hope, but with a Roberts torpedo carved on the front of the base. Headstones flanked it, and
the whole was surrounded by an elaborate stone fence, all supplied by Fullerton in 1873. Only
the headstones and the base of the central monument survive. (Drake Well Museum.)

BRYAN PLOT, WOODLAWN CEMETERY.
John C. Bryan's monument was also
provided by Fullerton in 1873. The
classical plain obelisk has been topped
with a cross and placed on a base with
arched tablets. Individual plots were
marked by lower cushionlike stones,
and the scrolled bases topped by urns
were footstones.

NEILL PLOT, WOODLAWN CEMETERY.
The Egyptian style, symbolizing
eternity, made its appearance in the
William T. Neill family monument
of 1876, where the central obelisk
was replaced by an Egyptian lotus
capital column.

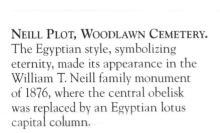

FAREL PLOT, WOODLAWN CEMETERY. The James Farel monument of the mid-1870s is a tour de force of marble cutting; the broken columns, symbolizing the broken relationships of death, are covered by a drape and tied with a tasseled cord.

MCKINNEY MAUSOLEUM, WOODLAWN CEMETERY. By the 1890s, more elaborate monuments came into fashion. James C. McKinney's 1897 mausoleum was the first, and one of the fancier, with its archaic Ionic columns and anthemia. It cost $20,000 and is cruciform in plan, surmounted by a large, banded dome.

FERTIG MAUSOLEUM, WOODLAWN CEMETERY. John Fertig's 1903 mausoleum is a plain classical Ionic temple situated on a promontory, fronted by terraces and steps. Others, the McKelvys, Carters, Charles Emersons, and Shanks, followed in the same basic mode.

BARNSDALL MAUSOLEUM, WOODLAWN CEMETERY. The largest mausoleum was constructed in 1903 by Theodore N. Barnsdall at a cost of $30,000. In the Egyptian style—closely resembling a Ptolemaic temple at Phylae—it has 24 vaults inside.

McKinney Plot, Woodlawn Cemetery. In 1894, John L. McKinney built this understated classical granite wall around his family plot, which has large flat individual markers. The bronze gate is missing.

Emerson Plot, Woodlawn Cemetery. The Paynes and E. O. Emersons preferred a central underground vault with inscriptions on the massive ashlar walls around their plots. The Emerson wall has inscribed panels and once had a bronze gate.

DRAKE MONUMENT, WOODLAWN CEMETERY. In 1901, oil millionaire Henry H. Rogers paid $100,000 for this handsome classical monument to Edwin L. Drake at the entry of Woodlawn Cemetery. Designed by Charles Brigham, the curving back wall with memorial inscriptions stands behind a semicircular bench, with veiled figures of Grief and Memory in low relief at each end. The central Ionic columns and pediment frame Charles Henry Niehaus's bronze statue *The Driller*, and the Drakes lie in front.

SEEP PLOT, ST. CATHARINE'S CEMETERY. Joseph Seep, seeing the need for a larger Roman Catholic cemetery then Calvary Cemetery south of town, donated the land for St. Catharine's Cemetery near Hydetown, and his family plot is marked by this monument in the Romanesque style, as his West Main Street home had been.

Five

PITHOLE NONRESIDENTIAL STRUCTURES

Pithole, or Pithole City, was founded in the narrow valley of Pithole Creek, about 15 miles southeast of Titusville, following large oil discoveries there in January 1865. Oil derricks filled the valley between Pithole in the west and smaller communities of Balltown and Prather City in the east. A. P. Duncan and George S. Prather bought the land in May and leased the city lots instead of selling them. Nonetheless, once leasing began almost two whole streets were lined with buildings within four days. The streets were never paved and remained tracks in the mud, although some planks were laid across parts of First and Holmden Streets.

The majority of the inhabitants were transients, living in hotels or boardinghouses. Supplying their needs were stores, eating houses, saloons, brothels, and three churches. The population grew to almost 15,000, prompting establishment of a post office in July 1865. The *Pithole Daily Record* began publication in September, and the town was incorporated in December. Although it met the basic needs of its inhabitants, the city was never substantial—there were no brick buildings—or particularly attractive. There was not even a proper cemetery; land adjacent to the Holmden family plot was used for some burials, but most who died were shipped home.

Pithole was isolated, and Samuel VanSyckle, tired of paying to haul oil barrels in wagons, laid the world's first oil pipeline in September 1865, connecting Pithole to Miller Farm. A railroad connection was made in March 1866.

The end was in sight, however. Early in 1866, oil production began to decline, and with it the population. Serious fires destroyed portions of the city, and in 1868, the three-year leases of city lots began to expire. Many residents moved to other towns, taking their buildings with them. Even the newspaper moved to Petroleum Center in May 1868. The 1870 census showed just 281 inhabitants, and only about 50 of the town's remaining buildings were in use. The borough charter was surrendered in 1877, and by 1895, only the cellar holes remained to indicate a city had ever been there.

CITY VIEW, 1865. Pithole at its height rose up from Pithole Creek, with Holmden Street at the bottom and Duncan Street, four blocks up, at the top of the hill. At the upper left, side by side on Duncan Street, are the United Presbyterian and Methodist churches. (Drake Well Museum.)

CITY VIEW, 20TH CENTURY. Taken from the southwest, this photograph shows how Pithole had evaporated. Instead of streets of buildings, the Methodist church stood alone at the top of the hill. (Drake Well Museum.)

HOLMDEN STREET. Construction was in progress in this view of Holmden Street near Second Street taken in the summer of 1865. On the left, the Metropolitan House, built by oilman J. J. Vandergrift, had stores on the ground floor and a tall false front above its plain windows. The Hubbs House, on the right, not one of Pithole's better hotels, had a Greek Revival doorway. The U.S. Drug Store, beyond it, was built with vertical boards on the sides, like a barn, and with a false front. (Drake Well Museum.)

PRATHER CITY. The Bonta House in Prather City, built by James W. Bonta, had 60 rooms, accommodating 175 people, and opened on January 1, 1866. Although it was a relatively plain wooden building, it had a balcony edged with wooden spindles all the way around the second floor, with French windows opening onto it. Salvage rights to its lumber were sold in a lottery won by Franklin Tarbell, and portions of the hotel reappeared in his Titusville mansion. (Drake Well Museum.)

DANFORTH HOUSE, FIRST AND HOLMDEN STREETS. The Danforth House stood at the corner of First and Holmden Streets, the very center of town. The three-story frame building had a first-floor veranda, a deep cornice, and a flat, Italianate roof. The windows had frames with slight pediments on top. Built by D. B. Danforth at a cost of $40,000 on a $14,000 lot, it opened on Christmas Eve 1865 and accommodated 140. (Drake Well Museum.)

NEAR FOURTH STREET. St. Patrick's Roman Catholic Church was smaller than its counterpart in Petroleum Center but featured similar arched windows. Founded by Fr. John L. Finucane, services began in December 1865. Regular masses ended in June 1866, but it was visited by Franciscan priests. Like many Pithole buildings, it was moved to Tionesta in 1886, long after the city was abandoned, and renamed St. Anthony's. (Drake Well Museum.)

METHODIST CHURCH, DUNCAN STREET. The Pithole Methodist Church, organized by Rev. Darius S. Steadman in 1865, constructed this frame building the same year. The side windows had flat wooden Gothic caps and the front an unusual entry with doors on each side of a vestibule, below an arched Gothic window. The belfry looks unfinished, and it may have been, as the church was sold by the sheriff in 1866. The building was described as 40 feet by 71 feet, with a steeple "about 45 feet" high and with a parsonage connected. (Drake Well Museum.)

INTERIOR, METHODIST CHURCH. This photograph purports to show the interior of the Methodist church about 1900, with a fancy stove, fresco borders on the walls above the wainscot, and pressback chairs on the front platform. There were six exposed roof timbers and 36 rows of oak pews. An architect by the name of Walter (?) Kemble designed both the Methodist and United Presbyterian churches. The church was abandoned in the 20th century and demolished in 1935. (Drake Well Museum.)

UNITED PRESBYTERIAN CHURCH, DUNCAN STREET. The 1865 Pithole United Presbyterian Church was also frame and resembled the Methodist church, although it had round-arched windows. Organized by Rev. George K. Ormond, it apparently never had a settled pastor. A sheriff's sale of its property in 1866 described the building as 40 feet by 60 feet, with a 20-foot tower with a 13-foot belfry. Moved to Oil City, it was rebuilt as Trinity Methodist and then served as Eagan's Grocery, seen here, before being demolished in 1955. (Drake Well Museum.)

FIRST AND HOLMDEN STREETS, 1895. This photograph, dated August 1895, shows the cellar hole of the Danforth House at right. The site was virtually cleared only 30 years after the city was founded. It was purchased in 1957 by the late James B. Stevenson, who removed the brush and opened the old roadways and then donated the land to the state in 1961. (Drake Well Museum.)

CHASE HOUSE, HOLMDEN STREET. The Chase House was completed in 1865 by George K. Chase at a cost of $100,000. The original portion (center) had a two-story veranda with stairs to the second floor. Inside were 132 rooms, with a saloon, and the Union Express and city post offices on the first floor. Above were the dining room, an exchange room, a reading room, and a ladies' lounge. The building was plain, but it was valuable enough to be moved to Pleasantville in 1868. (Drake Well Museum.)

NOS. 50–52 FIRST STREET. The Astor House, an absolutely plain wooden building, and nothing like its New York namesake, was only famous for having been built in one day. (Drake Well Museum.)

No. 45 Holmden Street. The Pithole Hotel, seen in this 1886 photograph, was a large two-story house, plain except for a spartan Greek Revival doorway with transom and side lights. (Drake Well Museum.)

First Street. Looking east across the valley toward Prather City, there are only derricks and plain utilitarian buildings, except for the Bonta House on the hill in the upper left. (Drake Well Museum.)

Six

PETROLEUM CENTER NONRESIDENTIAL STRUCTURES

Petroleum Center (originally Petroleum Centre) received its name from the fact that it developed on Oil Creek, about midway between Titusville and Oil City. In 1861, the Central Petroleum Company laid out Washington Street, the main thoroughfare of the new city, parallel to the west bank of the creek.

Petroleum Center shared many characteristics with Pithole; it developed at a major oil producing site, its buildings were almost entirely frame (one was brick), it rapidly grew to a city of 10,000, and it was rapidly abandoned as production began to decline in 1869. Its post office opened in 1864, and by 1865, the town boasted 25 hotels, as many saloons, and a theater. It always had better transportation than Pithole, since flatboats could use the creek, and there was a rail connection by 1865. The newspaper, moved from Pithole and renamed the *Petroleum Center Daily Record*, was published from May 1868 through November 1873. Like Pithole, the town had a reputation for wickedness, with saloons and brothels, but it also had three churches, so it was probably hyperbole when amateur bard A. S. Marsh wrote in 1869, "This place has long been noted for its Rowdies and their train, And People that did live there, have seemed almost Insane."

Like Pithole, the lots of Petroleum Center were leased, rather than sold, to residents, giving them little incentive to stay once the oil ran out. The city directory for 1872 still listed more than 1,000 residents, mostly laborers, but included oil operators, saloon keepers, lawyers, physicians, teamsters, confectioners, milliners, restaurateurs, several "old gents," and at least one "gambler." The town lasted into the 1880s, two of the churches remained in use past 1900, and a number of houses stood until demolished by the state in the 1960s when Oil Creek State Park was established. The McClintock family cemetery just north of town had no room for town burials; so a larger cemetery was laid out southwest of it. It was described as "behind the churches," so they apparently stood down the hill from it, toward Washington Street.

CITY VIEW, 1867. This panorama shows the more important buildings in the upper left center; the brick Bissell and Company bank rises above a sea of wooden buildings, and the three-story frame Central Hotel with its two-story veranda appears to its left along the railroad tracks. Above the bank is the Roman Catholic church, and to the right, the Presbyterian church. (Drake Well Museum.)

CITY VIEW, 1896. This panorama shows the same area 15 years later, and the city had evaporated. The Central Hotel burned in 1878, set on fire by sparks from the train. Other structures have been moved, demolished, or salvaged. (Drake Well Museum.)

CATHOLIC CHURCH. SS. Peter and Paul Roman Catholic Church was a substantial frame building, with arched doors and windows, a double arched belfry atop the central tower, and a rectory attached. It was established about 1866, and Fr. John L. Finucane served it along with Pithole that year. Fr. James J. Dunn was resident priest from 1868 to 1874. (Drake Well Museum.)

PRESBYTERIAN CHURCH. The Presbyterian Church was organized in September 1865, J. T. Oxtoby was elected pastor in 1868, and David Patton served from 1870 to 1872. The building was frame, with large shuttered windows and an octagonal cupola, and later housed a union congregation. A Methodist church, founded in 1863, stood near the cemetery, but no pictures of it appear to have survived. Its steps were visible in the 1950s. (Drake Well Museum.)

BISSELL AND COMPANY, WASHINGTON STREET. George H. Bissell and Company, bankers, paid $3,500 for a 99-year lease of a 60-foot-by-75-foot lot at the corner of Washington and Main Streets in 1867 and built this two-story brick bank. Its second-floor windows are identical—even the cast-iron caps—to those of the First and Second National Banks of Titusville, built the preceding year, indicating a preference, a limited selection, or perhaps both. The Bissell partners surrendered their lease for $1,000 in 1878, the building burned in 1921, and the bank's steps at the corner are all that remain. (Drake Well Museum.)

WASHINGTON STREET. This 1866 photograph shows the buildings stretching north along Washington Street. The corner of the Bissell Bank appears at left, taller than most of the other structures. Oil Creek was behind the buildings on the right. (Drake Well Museum.)

124

PETROLEUM CENTER. The unplanned nature of Petroleum Center is evident in this 1866 view. Tanks of the Central Petroleum Company are located across the street from the Lakeshore House hotel, and next to it was SS. Peter and Paul Church. (Drake Well Museum.)

CENTRAL HOTEL, MAIN STREET. The three-story Central Hotel, with its double veranda, resembled Pithole's Chase House, but it was fancier, with wooden scrollwork between the columns. (Drake Well Museum.)

CENTRAL PETROLEUM COMPANY, MAIN STREET. The offices of the Central Petroleum Company were functional buildings without any particular style. (Drake Well Museum.)

PETROLEUM CENTER CEMETERY. Bodies of those who died in Petroleum Center were usually shipped home for burial. In 1871, Lavina Wilcox, whom the *Petroleum Center Daily Record* described as "a woman of the town known as 'Whiskey Lu,'" died, and her friends paid for her funeral, hoping her burial there would be only temporary. Her medium-sized marble headstone, one of the few from the 1870s, is still in the cemetery.

INDEX

DISCOVER THOUSANDS OF LOCAL HISTORY BOOKS FEATURING MILLIONS OF VINTAGE IMAGES

Arcadia Publishing, the leading local history publisher in the United States, is committed to making history accessible and meaningful through publishing books that celebrate and preserve the heritage of America's people and places.

Find more books like this at
www.arcadiapublishing.com

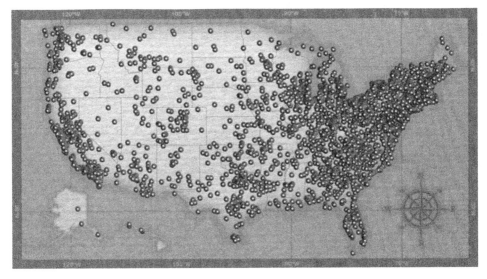

Search for your hometown history, your old stomping grounds, and even your favorite sports team.

Consistent with our mission to preserve history on a local level, this book was printed in South Carolina on American-made paper and manufactured entirely in the United States. Products carrying the accredited Forest Stewardship Council (FSC) label are printed on 100 percent FSC-certified paper.

MADE IN THE USA

CPSIA information can be obtained
at www.ICGtesting.com
Printed in the USA
BVOW03*2202171216
471137BV00024B/348/P